Gratitude

Your Master Key to Mindset Change

BOOK DIARY JOURNAL

Maria Burke

978-1-9993660-2-5

Names and identifying details have been changed to protect the privacy of individuals. Published in Ireland by Maria Burke Publishing.

This book is dedicated to my lovely daughter, Holly, and to my fantastic nieces and nephews, Katie, Rossa, Kyle, Ry-Lee, and Naoise, listed in order of age. I'm so grateful for the fun and adventure you all bring to my life, especially the cold-lake swims followed by Martin Murphy's delicious ice-cream.

Contents

Introduction

What they undertook to do
They brought to pass;
All things hang like a drop of dew
Upon a blade of grass.
— *Gratitude to the Unknown Instructors*, William Butler Yeats

Do you worry too much? Are you hard on yourself when things go wrong? Perhaps blame yourself even if it's not at all your fault? Does your brain regularly latch on to negative thoughts? Do you want to be kinder to others? Feel you're not as kind as you could be? Do you simply wish you had more fun, more joy in your life? Maybe you're frequently overwhelmed, constantly putting off doing stuff—tidying your desk, exercising more, eating healthier, asking for that salary increase—even though you know you'd feel better after doing it?

The secret to life and career success lies in arming yourself with practical, common-sense tools to improve your own wellbeing, no matter what your situation. Whether you're too busy and swamped, feeling lonely, isolated, or just a bit meh, the tools and habits outlined in this workbook will revive and renew so you can get your excitement and energy back to embrace life and your purpose.

Gratitude is, for me, the biggest key to mindset change, the primary tool I use to shift my brain from worry and procrastination to a state of calm and 'can-do'. Gratitude may seem 'soft and fluffy', not hard-hitting enough to help with life's challenges, such as increased workload, difficult relationships, and career decisions. But studies show that when practised regularly, gratitude is the powerful master key to unlocking mindset change, helping you get to the place where you focus better and make wiser decisions. My clients and I find that practicing gratitude creates a mindset that enables us to set clearer goals, better, and bigger goals that enable this improved focus and wiser decision-making. We also find gratitude extremely effective in finding that almost-instant spark to take the mind from a less positive to a positive 'can-do' place that's essential for the formation of good habits.

My granny showed me what a difference gratitude can make in our lives. She always seemed happy. She smiled, laughed a lot, and rarely complained about her fate. Yet her life hadn't been—and wasn't—easy. She grew up poor and her husband died before she was 50 years old, leaving her with a family of five young children to rear. Money, which had always been scarce, became even scarcer. By the time I was born, she was in her seventies, her hair snow white. She was crippled with arthritis, hardly ever left her countryside home in the West of Ireland, wore the same dark clothes and an apron almost every day, and had very few possessions—certainly none that weren't absolutely necessary.

As she grew older, and was less able to move about, she used to sit in her kitchen by the fire most days, with no TV, until she died in her late eighties. Neighbours and family came and went. She greeted everyone with a huge welcome and a big smile. When my two brothers and I were young, she always hid treats for us—Tayto crisps, Cadbury's chocolate bars, Lucozade, an assortment of jellies—behind the curtains and underneath the furniture. We absolutely loved visiting granny. Every Saturday morning, we pelted in the door, beating one another out of the way to get to the hidden goodies. We got to know the hiding places, so the finding part didn't take long, then we all settled down for a chat, while stuffing ourselves with our loot.

Granny always thanked everyone for coming to visit. She was grateful for a sunny day (in the West of Ireland, this was indeed something to be thankful for). When it rained—and it rained a lot—she always said we needed it to help the crops grow. She enjoyed sitting by the fire drinking lots of tea, perfectly content. Of course, as a child, I just accepted her outlook as her personality, never really thought about it. But now, as an adult, I think of her when I practice gratitude to help my clients and myself navigate life with a sense of calm, and to bring more joy. She was front of mind the entire time I worked on this book. Granny didn't have wealth or business success, yet, being *consistently* (more about consistency later) thankful for the simple things in life evidently helped her cope with life's up's and down's, not to mention bringing her happiness, laughter, and joy.

When I knew my granny, her life seemed simple, but most of our lives are not; they're busier, more complex. We often can't and don't wish to choose a life lived at home, waiting for people to come and go. In today's world, where we don't visit others at home as much as in the past, we could wait at home and it might well happen that nobody would visit for days, or even weeks. While today's trend of flexible work hours and working from home appeal to many, the practice can contribute to feelings of loneliness and isolation. Living in a hair-trigger global economy, with individual financial pressures causing increased stress, we can all, I believe, learn from my granny's story. Using gratitude as a tool in your tool kit for mental wellness is something that is available for everyone.

Whether you're rich or poor, too busy and overwhelmed with your long to-do list, lonely and isolated, feeling despondent, burned out, unmotivated, lacking meaning and purpose—whatever your own personal worry, practicing gratitude by thinking about (and even better, writing down) daily thoughts of what you're thankful for, fills your mind and body with a sense of peace, fulfilment, and even joy. It's a tremendously useful internal resource, helping you to reduce anxiety and stress and propelling you towards a more successful and fulfilling life.

This book can kick-start your own gratitude practice. Read the stories, review the evidence, take advantage of the exercises and tools to build your own formula for wellbeing, resilience, and purpose. To help you develop your gratitude practice and create more of what you are most grateful for in your life, I've devoted the second half of this workbook to the following pieces:

- **Your Routine 66 diary** (more about the name later) for you to write down your daily gratitude list and to help you on your journey towards your more grateful self.
- **Random Thoughts and Ideas journaling space** to use in whatever way benefits you the most—for ideas, insights, actions.

As you journey towards your more grateful self and experience the benefits being grateful brings you, I hope that reading this book will help you arrive in a place that's calmer, more productive, and joyful—full of purpose and meaning.

Part I

Gratitude: The Master-Key to Mindset Change

Gratitude makes sense of our past, brings peace for today, and creates a vision for tomorrow.

—*The Language of Letting Go: A Meditation Book and Journal for Daily Reflections,* Melody Beattie

I believe a complete tool kit is necessary for us to live our best lives. Gratitude is one powerful tool to help build resilience, cultivate calmness, and help you on the road to a more productive and contented life. The secret, as I mentioned, lies noting to yourself—and even better, consistently writing down—what you're grateful for.

Practicing gratitude to improve your day is one of the best self-care tools for achieving instant results when you need to be lifted from worry to calm and from feeling down to just that little bit better. The bigger benefits, such as being consistently kinder to yourself, setting clearer goals, and being more productive take regular practice. Results improve as you build the habit. The practice is simple and very effective. For lasting benefits, expressing gratitude is something that's best practised daily for at least two months until it becomes a useful habit, an action you will automatically fall back on when you need it.

Why two months?

Phillippa Lally, a health psychology researcher at University College London, is well known for her research about how long it takes to form a new habit. Prior to Lally's research, it was believed that it took 21 days to form a new habit. Nice, right? Very do-able. Not too long to try something that might work.

But, as it turns out, it's not quite that easy. Lally observed the habits of 96 people during a 12-week period. Each participant chose *one* new daily habit, one action they carried out at the same time every day. Volunteers reported daily on whether they carried out the task and, if so, how automatic this new behaviour felt.

Various actions included drinking a bottle of water with lunch, running for 15 minutes before dinner, and eating a piece of fruit with lunch. At the end of the 12 weeks, the researchers studied the data to determine how long it took each person to transition from starting a new behaviour to that behaviour becoming 'automatic'.

Studies show that the time it takes to develop a new habit can vary widely depending on the behaviour, the person, and the circumstances.[1] In Lally's study, it took anywhere from 18 to 254 days for people to form a new habit, with 66 days being the average—more than the previously accepted 21 days, yet still very do-able when you decide to take action.

My own experience with forming a gratitude habit was that initially I found when I expressed gratitude my mindset switched from worried to positive immediately. When I started consistently writing down what I was grateful for, I experienced more lasting benefits such as feeling better about myself, clarity of thought and increased focus became the norm rather than the exception.

What's stopping you? Sixty-six days will pass anyway. If you want or need an improvement in certain areas of your life, why not start with deciding to make one small change now to help you get that improvement. Think of gratitude as your master key to open the door to any positive change you want or need in your life.

When we receive gratitude, when we feel gratitude, and most important, when we express gratitude, our brain releases the neurotransmitters dopamine and serotonin, both of which are necessary for the 'feel-good factor'. These chemicals improve our mood immediately. We feel happier, more creative, and in the right mindset to take the steps toward needed changes in our lives.

The Five Thank You's

One very simple daily routine, and a great place to start your gratitude practice, is incorporating something I call the *Daily Five Thank You's* into your daily schedule.

You can say your *Five Thank You's* throughout the day, whenever it suits you, wherever you need to—any time you feel that changing your current thinking pattern would benefit your day. In the beginning, while the habit is forming, I recommend choosing a specific time every day and setting a reminder. Before you start the practice, decide what time of day would benefit you most. Practicing gratitude at least once each day is a baseline. There may be times when you want to practice more than that—absolutely, go for it.

You may choose the morning, when you wake up, before you even get out of bed, to say thank you for the things in your life that you appreciate. Keep this list simple: perhaps be grateful for a good night's sleep, the comfy bed, that you organised your work schedule and your clothes last night. The items you select don't have to be complicated or deep. The action of switching your mind to an outlook of gratitude means that your day instantly starts on a more positive note. Perhaps, if you've had a sleepless night, take a brisk walk, eat a nice breakfast, or savour that first coffee before you list your *Five Thank You's*.

On the weekdays, I say my *Five Thank You's* as I walk or drive to work. I've practiced gratitude at this time of days for years, and, oh boy, it makes all the difference in my outlook, changes the tone for my day from morning-grouch-mood to a more positive one! I started the habit in my mid-twenties when I was running my own pharmacies. Business was challenging. I had cashflow difficulties. Interest rates were extremely high, so loans were out of the question. And I had no idea how to lead and motivate my team for better results. I was learning by my mistakes (plenty of opportunity) and finding it difficult to cope.

On top of that, unable to afford a good car, I drove an old Volkswagen Beetle with a hole in the floor under where I placed my right foot when driving. When it rained or when I drove through a puddle, my foot got soaked. This same car didn't do well on hills unless I built up enough speed to take a good run at them. One hill became a real problem. It's in the middle of Dublin city, en route to my work at the time—a busy route. If I needed to stop on this hill at a red traffic signal, I almost always had to get out and push (in the never-ending rain) to start the car again, depending on the kindness of strangers to help get up and over the hill. My job, my finances—it was all getting me down. I read somewhere that practicing gratitude would help, so I started searching my brain for the good things in my life.

I started to say 'thank you' for at least five things a day, and I did this, two to three times every day—on the way to work, on the drive home, and sometimes late at night too. Advice in the myriad self-help books and articles I read was to keep it simple, so I did. I said 'thank you' for a good night's sleep, the first lovely cup of tea in the morning (the first cup is always the best), a sunny day, an interesting conversation, after my car got up and over that big hill, and any exercise I managed to fit in. If I ran early that morning, I said 'thanks' for that. If I didn't run, I said 'thanks' for the extra half hour in bed. You'll always find stuff to be grateful for if you choose to do so.

When listing *Five Thank You's*, it's important to be 100 percent truthful with yourself and only say 'thank you' for things you're truly grateful for. There's nobody you need to impress with this. For the morning thank you's, I've discovered it's helpful to be specific and not get into generalities that we can all recite when we don't have time to think of the best answer. We may definitely be thankful for our families, friends, and being alive, but my it's more beneficial to your practice to be specific about what you're grateful in the moment. It not only improves the moment, but it increases awareness. Usually there are slightly different things to be grateful for each day, by being specific, within a few days, you'll widen the lens of all you have in your life that's truly wonderful. Being specific also helps you recognise patterns in your gratitude as time goes by, especially if you write down what you're thankful for so you can easily track these things. Hugs, exercise, a tasty coffee, meeting special friends—can all remind you of what you'd like to do more of in your life. For instance, a client of mine told me that she often says thank you for escaping being awakened during the night by a snoring husband, thus getting a proper night's sleep!

Opportunity to reflect: List 5 things you're grateful for right now—today

1. ______________________________

2. ______________________________

3. ______________________________

4. ______________________________

5. ______________________________

In addition to choosing a particular time each day, taking a breath and switching to gratitude any time you feel stressed or under pressure can calm you, ground you in the moment, and elevate your mood. During a particularly stressful workday, it's good to find a space away from your desk, perhaps out of your home or office, take a few deep breaths, and remind yourself of the good things that happened that day. There will always be a few.

The *Five Thank You's* are also extremely effective for unwinding at the end of the day. You know how tough it can be. Sometimes at night, when you're tired, stress and unhappiness can hit. Or after an especially busy day, when you're weary, your mind won't calm down. Before going to bed, writing down and then repeating the *Five Thank You's* can help lift your mood, calm your mind, and help you get to sleep more easily.

In a study by a group of researchers in China looking at the combined effects of gratitude and sleep quality on symptoms of anxiety and depression, it was found that higher levels of gratitude were associated with better sleep, and with lower anxiety and depression.[2]

After a few days of listing the *Five Thank You's*, no matter how stressful your life, you'll realise there's something every day to be grateful for—things like an enjoyable phone call from a friend, a tasty dinner, a lovely hot shower, a laugh with a colleague. Perhaps you overcame a challenge, helped a co-worker, or organised your desk. Even in stressful times, it's possible to find moments to be thankful for—you simply must choose to do so.

Friends, clients, and colleagues tell me they rely on this tool when they feel particularly fed up with life, and that within a very short time, not only does expressing gratitude become a habit, but they start appreciating life again, which makes the hard times easier. One client told me that logging daily in a gratitude diary whilst going through her divorce helped keep her sane. Try it and see. This practice takes very little time out of your day and the beauty of it is, the more you do it, the more benefits such as improved mindset and positivity as well as starting to worry less, you'll see.

Patterns: There to Be Noticed

Another benefit of the daily *Five Thank You's* surprised me. After a few weeks of reciting or writing down my list—either en route to work or at night—I noticed a pattern emerging of what type of things I was grateful for. I was always thankful for any bit of exercise I did that day, especially if it was outdoors, so I started to make sure to include outdoor exercise as often as possible. Within a few weeks I had doubled the amount of outdoor exercise I did. As those happiness-inducing endorphins kicked in, many aspects of my life improved: I was more effective at work and started to enjoy my job. I coped with stressful situations better. I became easier to be around and, therefore, felt less worn-out at the end of each day.

In Part II of this book, you'll find friendly prompts to encourage you to notice the patterns emerging in your gratitude. This will help you really recognise what you'd like to do more of. You'll see the evidence for yourself.

Before I started the *Five Thank You's*, I would have expected to be thankful for the chocolate treats I ate every day. Perhaps because I worry about weight-gain, there's often that little bit of guilt associated with cakes and treats for me, so I tend not to include these in my gratitude lists. In later years, when I noticed the emerging pattern of being thankful for hugs from my daughter—often the first thing I say thank you for every night—I make sure to give and get plenty of these every day. I still do.

Overcoming challenges is also something I noticed appearing in my gratitude list. When I ran my health and beauty distribution company, and dealt with leading global brands and major customers, I'd become stressed before buyer meetings, sales meetings, and often before brand contract negotiations. Yet after these meetings had passed successfully, and for the most part things had gone well, I started to list each successful outcome in my journal as something to be grateful for. After a couple of months, I came to realise that I didn't need to be so stressed before these meetings. I just needed to prepare well, so that I felt calmer and more optimistic about the meetings! I focused more on the positive feelings of gratitude afterwards. In doing so, I changed how my brain approached the challenges, and I became calmer and more effective.

The *Five Thank You's* was the first self-development tool I ever used. It helped me so much that for many years now I've shared it with great success with friends and colleagues. Since I began coaching, I've found that when clients work with *The Five Thanks You's* they very shortly start to become less overwhelmed, sleep better, and feel calmer. They find more joy in life. There's nothing to lose by giving gratitude a try—and so much to be gained. The magic happens when you do it, when you take time to be thankful consistently.

When you decide to practice gratitude on a regular basis, you might sometimes forget. If this happens, don't be hard on yourself. Be grateful whenever saying the *Five Thank You's* comes to mind. You'll feel the benefits and the decision to continue the practice will come. With consistency comes the magic. You live life from a better place within yourself and perceived problems are easier to cope with.

Studies by UCLA's Mindfulness Awareness Research Centre show that regularly expressing gratitude alters the molecular structure of the brain, keeps the grey matter working, and makes us healthier and happier. Carrie D. Clarke, International Management Consultant explains it clearly in a *Thrive Global* article: 'The practice of gratitude increases your dopamine production which encourages your brain to seek out more of the same. It's the brain saying, "Oh, do that again," which means the more you're grateful for, the more you will *find* to be grateful for. Some say, "what you appreciate, appreciates." On a scientific level, this is an example of Hebb's Law, which states "neurons that fire together wire together."[3]

So, what's stopping you?

The Pen Is Mighty

Research shows that people who very vividly describe (in written form) or picture their goals are anywhere from 1.2 to 1.4 times as likely to successfully accomplish their goals than those who don't.[4]

Writing down what you're grateful for will enhance the effectiveness of your gratitude work.

In the workbook section of this book, you'll find prompts, and plenty of space to add to your descriptions of what you're grateful for, and to describe more vividly the benefits that recognizing and recording gratitude are delivering for you. You will then be able to draw on this information to make more informed decisions that improve aspects of your life and work.

I found this to be true when I wrote my first book *The Formula: How to Live Your Very Best Life.* As the process developed, writing, reading, editing, over and over, my own habits improved. I drank more water, exercised consistently, recited positive affirmations, and worked more to my strengths and values—all because I was reading and writing about these every day. Life essentially became better.

Building Relationships and Advancing Your Career

The obligation to express gratitude deepens with procrastination. The longer you wait, the more effusive must be the thanks.

—*Miss Manners Rescues Civilization*, Judith Martin

In Marshall Goldsmith's wonderful, bestselling book *What Got You Here Won't Get You There*, he explains that thanking works because it expresses one of our most basic emotions: gratitude. He refers to saying 'thank you' as a necessary skill and an asset for building relationships and enhancing your career. He cites its absence as a major interpersonal flaw. I 100 percent agree.[5]

How many times have you said to yourself, 'I must say thank you' to someone for something they did for you, but you never got around to it? It's never too late. How great do you feel when someone thanks you (and you know they really mean it) for something you did for them? How wonderful is it to receive a card or note with a few thoughtful lines thanking you for your time, your effort, or a gift that's valued? Thank someone today, knowing they'll appreciate it, knowing you'll be making someone's day better.

When my daughter was younger, after every Christmas and birthday, I developed the habit of getting her to sit down with paper, markers, stickers, and all sorts of sparkly, fluffy, and other motivating card decorations to make thank you cards for gifts received from grandparents, aunts, and uncles. Lucky for her, her birthday and Christmas fall together, so she could send both thank you's in one card. Making and writing those cards was also a great way to pass time on a rainy afternoon. Now that she's a teenager, I don't need to tell her to thank people for the gifts they give her or the nice things they do for her. She sends thank you messages by phone now, yet every so often, she'll still make or buy a card to send. By encouraging your children to develop the skill of gratitude, properly, you'll be teaching them to connect with and appreciate others, which of course, can only be a good thing!

Opportunity for Action

Take this opportunity to list five people who have helped you, and to whom you'll send a thank you note today:

1. ______________________________

2. ______________________________

3. ______________________________

4. ______________________________

5. ______________________________

Now, I suggest putting down this book and sending those notes instead of reading further.

Gratitude and Resilience: The Connection

This quote from Rachel Hartman's young adult novel *Seraphina* always makes me smile: "Did I become court composer through masterful procrastination? Hardly!"[6] There's no doubt about it, to be good at anything—even gratitude—takes effort. No matter what skill you want to improve, it's likely you'll need to find the resilience to continue your practice from time to time.

Life is complex. It can be tough. No matter how successful you are, life is full of challenges. Whether it's in the area of health, career, relationships—anything—life has its ups and downs. Some people cope well, others not so well. Those who are the most resilient do best. The good news is that resilience is a character trait that can be learned.[7]

Being grateful helps to quickly change your mindset from feeling down about what's bothering you to thinking positively about what's good in your life. Right now. If you're someone who's hard on yourself when things go wrong, here's the good news: When you feel gratitude, you're not beating yourself up; your mind is in a different place, a better place, where you can start to build resilience. Try this: When you notice you're being hard on yourself and feeling that you can't cope. Stop. Take a few breaths. List in your mind (or better still on paper), your *Five Thank You's*.

Opportunity for Action

Take the opportunity to list the small stuff (below) that you're thankful for right now, today.

1. ____

2. ____

3. ____

4. ____

5. ____

You can use this gratitude list, or your lists in your 66-Day Gratitude Habit Diary as a reminder of what's going well in your life. You can congratulate yourself on the good stuff instead of being hard on yourself. Changing how you view things and reminding yourself of what's going well can help you pick yourself up when things are tough.

The Five Dollar Difference

It has been well said that our anxiety does not empty tomorrow of its sorrows, but only empties today of its strength.

—*The Salt-Cellars,* Charles Spurgeon

What do you do when you don't feel grateful for anything right now?

Sometimes, everything can feel as though it's going wrong. You're in a whirlwind of stress. You're overwhelmed, and you perhaps feel that there's nowhere you can go, no one who'll listen to your woes. You may even feel guilty about feeling so down. After all, logic tells you there are many people whose lives are worse than yours. Yet you can't seem to snap yourself out of your funk. What can you do when you don't feel like being thankful for anything?

The absolute best thing you can do is get out for a 40-minute run, brisk walk, or whatever type of aerobic exercise suits you. Really, movement is the most effective option to clear your head. If you decide the aerobic exercise is a 'no' for you at a particular time, for whatever reason, try doing what I recommend to my clients: think of something nice you can do for someone else. Doing so can snap you out of feeling sorry for yourself. It's that straightforward. Of course, it's okay to feel sorry for yourself sometimes. Most people do. But if it's a regular occurrence, you want to break that habit. Focusing on what you can do for others takes your train of thought to a different place. Take a deep breath, think of someone you can help, plan how to go about it, and then act.

Opportunity for Action

Write down five actions you can take to help someone else and note how these actions will help him or her:

1. ____

2. ____

3. ____

4. ____

5. ____

How do you think you'll feel after helping this person? I suggest you put a deadline date beside each action above, so you know you're committed.

When my daughter was about five years old, she asked me why she felt even more excited when she gave a gift to someone than when she received one. She's not alone. Friends have told me stories of their children bubbling with excitement as they waited for other family members to open the gift they got them. In fact, research shows that we may get longer-lasting happiness by giving to others, rather than receiving for ourselves.

Studies conducted in 2018 by psychologists Ed O'Brien and Samantha Kassirer[8] from the University of Chicago Booth School of Business and Northwestern University Kellogg School of Management involved a series of experiments to find which brought the longest-lasting joy—giving a gift to yourself or giving to others. In one of the experiments, 96 participants received five dollars every day for five days. Participants and were randomly designated to either spend the five dollars on themselves or on someone else, which could take the form of leaving money in a tip jar at a café or making an online donation to charity every day, but they had to spend the money on the exact same thing each day.

The findings showed that when participants repeatedly gave to others, their happiness did not decline, and the joy they felt from giving to others on the fifth day was just as strong as it was on the first. Those who spent money on themselves reported a steady decline in happiness over a 5-day period.

O'Brien and Kassirer carried out a second experiment online, which allowed them to keep the actions consistent across volunteers. This time, 502 volunteers played 10 rounds of a word puzzle game. They won $0.05 per round, which they either kept or donated to a charity of their choice. After each round, volunteers revealed the extent to which winning made them feel happy, elated, and joyful. Again, the self-determined happiness of those who gave their winnings away declined far more slowly than did the happiness reported by those who kept their winnings.

So, by now, even after learning the evidence, if you haven't already mentally committed to taking action, I suggest you go back and complete any gratitude exercises you may have skipped . . .

What to Do When You're Stuck

Sometimes you need help remembering what gratitude feels like to get to that place of feeling thankful.

Connect with the Feeling of Gratitude

I suggest repeating these steps until you find at least five things in your life to be grateful for.

1. First, get comfortable. Either sit or lie down in your own space. It doesn't have to be a quiet space. It can even be in an airport while waiting for your flight to board, on a bus, in your local park—anywhere you can close your eyes for a few minutes. Now close your eyes.
2. Take a few breaths with your attention on your breathing to clear your mind.
3. Think back to a time when you felt happy, successful, or grateful, a time in your personal or professional life when you felt on top of the world. Maybe it was when you achieved your goal and believed in yourself. Maybe you felt fulfilled and satisfied just being with someone special or doing something special, playing with your child in the garden, or reading a wonderful book—time you're glad happened in your life, when you felt joy. This time can be big or small—it just needs to be meaningful to you.
4. Open your eyes, find your pen and write about the circumstances of that event. If more than one event comes to mind, focus on the first one you thought of. Or if both hold equal weight, you can go through this exercise for each one.

What you were doing exactly?

What factors contributed to your success, happiness, and joy?

Who were you with? Did others play a part? Write more about the experience of feeling happy and content or perhaps feeling filled with excitement and a sense of purpose.

How exactly did you feel? What need or desire was fulfilled?

How and why did the experience give your life meaning and purpose?

What other factors contributed to your feeling of fulfilment?

Describe vividly what exactly you were grateful for because of this experience. (Repetition is okay here. Writing things down more than once helps embed the memories).

Because of what you are now reminded of, what immediate action will you take to reclaim those positive feelings?

By now, your mindset will be in a place more conducive to feeling gratitude. If it isn't, keep repeating this exercise until your perspective shifts—and it will. Keep listing five things you're grateful for. Remember, this exercise is to remind you how being grateful makes you feel, so you can feel that way once more. It's not about travelling back in time.

Again, you can start with small things you're grateful for. Why not be thankful you're taking time to read about gratitude. Or be grateful you're planning to use this tool to improve your life. Appreciate a sunny day. Think, think, think. There will be five small things you can be thankful for.

Let's Talk Practicalities

Accept periods of suffering with gratitude, knowing that suffering can teach you very important lessons.

—*Self-Meditation: 3,299 Tips, Quotes, Reminders, and Wake-Up Calls for Peace and Serenity,* Barbara Ann Kipfer

Because it's necessary to build internal resources with a practical toolkit to cope well with life's ups and downs, I've included a few more tools to help you. These are tips and tools my clients and I find valuable to help with making choices, setting the right goals, and relaxing. Use these tools in tandem with your gratitude practice, both to support your practice and to help with prioritising and goal setting.

Yes/No?

Make space in your life to develop habits for your wellbeing by using this straightforward practical tool to help your decision making. We're all responsible for our choices, and the choices we make determines the outcomes of our actions. This simple *Yes/No?* tool helps to prioritise and make wise choices. Just ask yourself, 'If I say *Yes* to this option, what am I saying *No* to?' When you're practicing gratitude, noticing the patterns, and determining what makes you feel the most grateful, you can use the *Yes/No?* tool to make sure you're on track. For example, if you feel like slacking off for an hour to watch one of your favourite shows, ask yourself, 'If I say *Yes* to an hour of TV, what am I saying *No* to? Exercise, meditation, gratitude-journaling, a relaxing bath, time with my family, socialising, preparing for tomorrow'?

I use the *Yes/No?* tool to ensure I exercise (health is one of my most important values). So, if I find myself debating about exercising, I ask myself, 'If I say *No* to a run or yoga, what am I saying *Yes* to'? Most likely, it's a less productive day and too much chocolate. You might ask yourself, 'If I say *Yes* to working late, what am I saying *No* to? 'If I say *Yes* to meeting this co-worker who tends to knock on my door just as I'm finishing up for the day, what am I saying *No* to? 'If I say *Yes* to writing in my gratitude journal today, what am I saying *No* to? Feeling miserable'?

If you're feeling a bit off but can't pinpoint the exact cause, a really great way to use this tool is to write down answers to this question: 'What's bugging me'? List possible causes, then perform the *Yes/No?* exercise with the items in the list to determine what's truly bothering you. For example, let's say you're a leader trying to get into the habit of working from home one day each week so you can catch up on correspondence, plan, read, and think. You haven't been managing to do this, and you're feeling overwhelmed. I find that many leaders are too busy during the workday to tend to strategic planning and to finding thinking time. It's quite a common challenge for busy people. Use the *Yes/No?* tool to clearly define what you're denying yourself and your team by continuing to say *No* to this one day to catch up. Are you saying *Yes* to personal and team stress because you, as a leader, are overwhelmed? Are you saying *Yes* to demotivated team members because you don't plan and delegate? What else are you saying *Yes* to by continuing to say *No* to what you really need? Why not use one of the Random Thoughts pages at the end of this workbook whenever you need it, so you'll have the details of what's bothering you to hand along with your gratitude work.

Meditation

Another tool to have in your kit is meditation, which, done regularly, can intensify the benefits of your gratitude practice. Contrary to what many of us have been brought up to believe, looking after our own needs is not selfish. A happy person—one who doesn't live life by sacrifice and denial—has more to offer family, friends, and colleagues. A martyr who always puts himself or herself last, does everything for everyone, then constantly complains of being worn out is no fun at all. They drain themselves and others. And martyrdom can lead to isolation as others probably won't seek out your company if you complain too much. A happy mum, dad, colleague, boss, or friend who is spreading support, love, and joy is a lot more fun to have around. Meditation can help hugely with your wellbeing and focus, and it's not as difficult as you may think to build a beneficial, enjoyable meditation habit.

Scientific research has revealed how meditation helps transform the brain and promote wellbeing.[9] People who meditate report feeling calmer, sharper, more creative, and more productive. They're better at problem solving and at letting things that don't matter roll off their backs. If you decide to try to meditate, to start your practice, I suggest you take five minutes each morning to meditate, then build your meditation time as you see the benefits. I know that most of us rush through many tasks every morning and time is tight. Believe me, it's worth getting out of bed ten minutes earlier than you usually do to take yourself to a quiet corner of your house, hotel room—wherever you are, even outside if it's available to you and weather permits. At night before going to sleep is also a lovely time to meditate, to bring calm to your mind and body and improve sleep.

As you meditate, notice as thoughts come and go. And they will. Try not to latch on to these thoughts, just let them float by. Be gentle with yourself as you explore this meditative practice. As you learn to let the thoughts go, your brain will become calmer, your mind freer of intrusive thoughts, and you are indeed meditating.

Through the Archway: A Guided Meditation to Help you Relax

This chakra meditation is a lovely practice to help you relax your mind—day or night. I find it wonderful, especially at night. Using images can help take your mind away from worry and stress. And it's easier to feel gratitude when you relax.

I have used this meditation myself, with my daughter to help her sleep, and with clients for relaxation. It's beautiful and works well for adults and children. I find that rubbing a child's forehead whilst gently talking through the meditation helps bring sleep. When your children sleep, they're happier, and you get more time to yourself. Actually, this meditation can be a two-in-one solution, because by the time you've guided your child to sleep, you become calm and relaxed too!

1. Find a comfortable space, either sitting in a chair, on a pillow, or in bed—wherever suits you. Just so long as you can sit up straight or lie down comfortably.

2. Close your eyes. Take your brain to somewhere you really love—a place where you're perfectly content and happy. Be in that place for a moment. Appreciate the space. Be happy there. A little smile may come to your face as you enjoy being there.
3. As you experience that lovely place, you notice an archway you've never seen before. You're curious. You wander slowly to the archway and walk through.
4. Once you're through the archway, you arrive in the most beautiful meadow filled with red flowers. You see red roses, poppies, and tulips. The earth beneath your feet is red. There are red apples growing on trees. The warm sun is setting, and the sky has a reddish hue. You have never seen such a beautiful red space in your life. As you walk barefoot on the soft red earth, the red colour gives you energy. You feel happy and content in this wonderful place. Take whatever time you desire to enjoy this feeling.
5. You come to a gate. You would like to see what's on the other side of the gate. You open the gate and walk through. You are now in an orchard filled with orange trees. You have never, ever, seen so many oranges in one place. The scent of oranges fills the air. You breathe in the lovely fresh aroma of the oranges. Orange tulips are growing at the base of the orange trees and the earth beneath your feet is covered in orange petals. The sky has turned a magnificent orange colour. You notice a picnic blanket with orange cushions and orange juice laid out there. You drink a glass of orange juice. It's the most delicious orange juice you have ever tasted. As you drink the

tasty juice and look at your beautiful orange surroundings, you notice an archway. Slowly, you wander toward it.

6. Through this gate is a field of yellow with a bright yellow sun shining down. You have arrived in a field full of primroses, sunflowers, tulips, daffodils, yellow lilies—a blanket made from every yellow flower you can imagine. You see your favourite type of flowers and walk slowly towards them. The ground beneath you is covered in soft yellow petals. There's a scent of lemon in the air. You look up, and in the distance, you see a lemon grove. You feel clear-headed and content as you wander slowly through the field of yellow. Now you see yet another archway. You walk towards it and through to the other side.
7. You are now in a huge green field with tall green grass growing there. You are at the top of the field, which rolls gently downhill. You sit down in the long grass and breathe in the fresh green-grass scent. You have an urge to roll down the hill, through the grass the way you did when you were a child. Off you go. You feel young, free, and ecstatic as you roll down the hill through the green grass.
8. You land on a fabulous beach with a twinkling blue sea at your feet. You look towards the horizon. The sky is so blue you can't make out where the sea and sky meet. The sun is shining in the clear blue sky. It's deliciously hot. You decide to go for a swim. As you float, free from care in the sparkly water, you enjoy being there, surrounded by blue sea and blue sky. As you swim along, you notice a shimmery purple light coming from a cave in the rocks. You swim to the cave.

9. Inside the cave is the most amazing formation of bright purple stalactites and stalagmites lit by a wonderful purplish light. You stand and gaze in wonder around the cave. The purple light gives you a calm, relaxed, sleepy feeling. You would like to lie down and snooze.
10. You notice a patch of pale, soft sand underneath a hole in the top of the cave. A gentle white light shines through. The sand is warm from the white sunlight shining down upon it. You lie there. The white light surrounds you, gently heating your body. As you breathe in and out in the white light, you start to gently doze. You're calm and relaxed.

Are you relaxed yet? Nearly there?

Setting Goals

My friend once told me that setting goals is like making pancakes. They're easy to prepare, you often make too many, and afterwards, you always think that a few well-made ones rather than too many sloppy ones would have been much better.

Setting the right goals makes it easier for you to act, and taking the right action is absolutely necessary for improved outcomes. I have included a piece on goal setting here that you can use to help with any goal you have in mind—including building a gratitude habit, the achievement of which is something I aim to help you with in this book. Be sure to express gratitude for each step you take towards achieving the goals you set, and indeed for anything you learn along the way.

Setting goals will not only help you with your gratitude habit but also with noticing patterns and translating them into a formula to improve your mindset and your chances for success.

The following tools will help you set and achieve your goals. You can start using them anytime—now, while you're completing your 66-Day Gratitude Habit Diary, and after. I use all these tools, as do many of my clients. Sometimes I use just one at a time, and sometimes I use two or three. Each person is unique, so play with them to determine which works best for you.

The Seven Principles of Setting a Well-Made Goal

Follow these principles to get you started and throughout your gratitude journey.

1. Ensure the goal you're working on is a passion, something you *really* want to achieve.
2. Make sure your new goal does not conflict with any of your other goals.
3. Develop goals in at least four areas of your life:
    a. Family and home
    b. Financial and career
    c. Health
    d. Social
4. Write your goal in the positive instead of the negative (I will ___________. I am doing _________.) Write your goal in detail, using vivid descriptions and to include sensory elements such as what you will see, hear, and feel when you reach it. Include the benefits of achieving your goal.

For example:

Every Friday I host a weekly 15-minute call with each member of my sales team, where we review numbers week and month to date, as well as, support needed, challenges ahead and we plan for next week. Our communication is clear, benefits everyone, and the meetings end with achievable plans. We all begin our weekend feeling positive and with a sense of purpose.

or

I'm running every morning for 20 minutes before work. I see the blue sky, feel the fresh air. I find my creativity and I begin each workday full of energy.

5. Think BIG. You can break down a goal into small steps to achieve the bigger goal.
6. Write down your timetable for both short-term and long-term goals. Deadlines are key. Monitor your progress regularly to make sure you act to ensure success.
7. Set goals that matter to you. When you set goals that really matter to you, you'll have a much better chance of achieving them.

Your GATSA Goal Setting Template

Use this template to help you think more clearly and to aid your decision-making, perhaps and to help you properly set-up your gratitude goal. I developed this template to provide clients with a formula that can be used for setting both short-term and long-term goals, with space to clarify the benefits of achieving the goal and to commit to actions. Clients find it especially useful with setting daily and weekly goals and with decision-making. Plus, it's short enough to use to prioritise daily and weekly tasks.

The template consists of five actions:

1. Set your **G**oal.
2. Determine an **A**chievable deadline.
3. **T**ake action and measure progress.
4. Imagine how achieving your goal will affect your **S**enses—what can you taste, touch, feel, smell, and see?
5. Think about how you see yourself **A**cting after achieving your goal. You'll do these last two steps from the moment you set your goal.

This template is especially effective when you're feeling a lack of focus or need to get on with prioritising, decision-making, and setting the right goals, many of which will be built on the patterns of what you're grateful for.

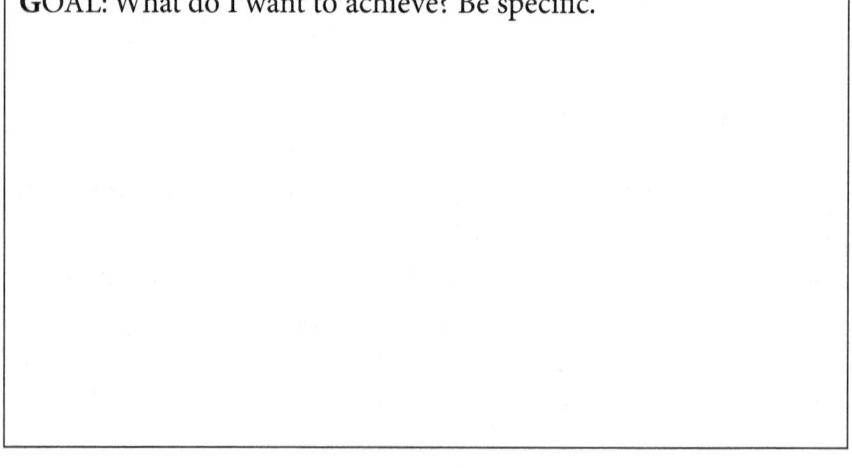

GOAL: What do I want to achieve? Be specific.

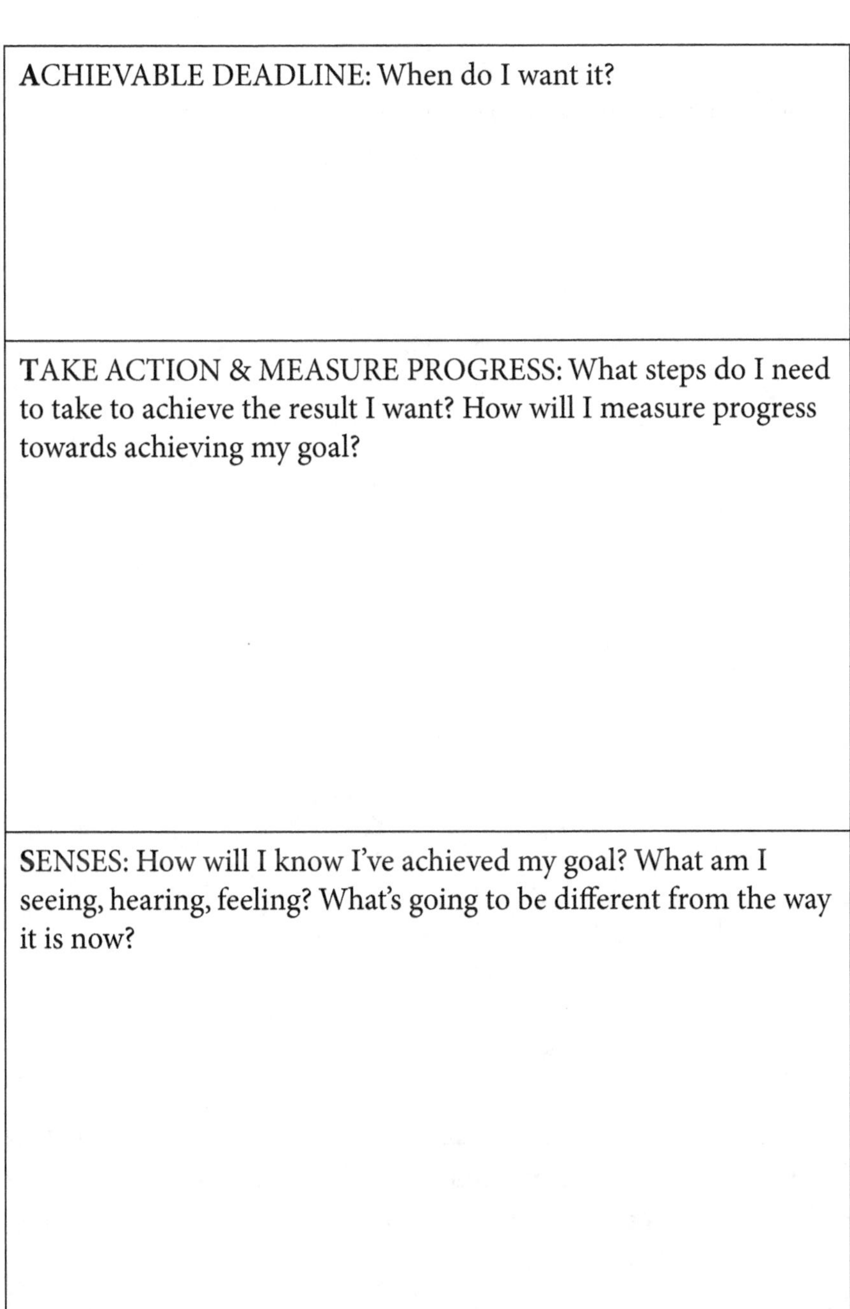

ACHIEVABLE DEADLINE: When do I want it?

TAKE ACTION & MEASURE PROGRESS: What steps do I need to take to achieve the result I want? How will I measure progress towards achieving my goal?

SENSES: How will I know I've achieved my goal? What am I seeing, hearing, feeling? What's going to be different from the way it is now?

ACTING DIFFERENTLY: What am *I* doing differently *now*, taking responsibility for, so that it's happening—I'm reaching my goal?

1.

2.

3.

4.

5.

Tip: Fill in this goal-setting template at the start of every day or every week to help you set clear, deliverable goals.

Questions and Options: Another Tool

Keep these questions handy for problem solving and building the resilience to keep moving towards your goals.

1. What's bugging you right now in your life? What problem do you have? Write it down in detail here. Keep it simple. For example, I'm out of my depth at work, or I'm behind in paying my mortgage, or I'm lonely. If you need help prioritising your problems and challenges, you can list everything that comes to mind and use the *Yes/No?* tool to determine which is most pressing.

____

____

____

____

____

____

2. Now, draw on your imagination and write here every solution you can think of—even options you'll never implement. This is crucial for you to see all the possibilities. Just write them down, don't make any decisions. You can write your options here, in your workbook, or (and this can be a fun and effective way to brainstorm) get some Post-its, write one possibility on each Post-it, and stick them on your wall.

____

____

3. Study all the options you've written down and reflect on the advantages and disadvantages of each one. If you opted for Post-its, you may even decide to organise your potential solutions into categories, such as easy, difficult, short-term fixes, gut-reaction. Take some time with this exercise.

4. When you have reflected on all the possibilities that are open to you, begin to choose. No option may be perfect, and you may not be 100 percent satisfied, but choose at least one that you are prepared to act on. Now, it's action-time. Write down what you're going to do and when.

Do It: Take Action

Tip: If you experience any wobbly moments while setting goals, you can refer to the gratitude lists you've already created. Later, while filling out your 66-Day Gratitude Habit Diary, you can revisit those gratitude lists to remind you of what's good in your life and to give you strength of purpose.

In the introduction, I mentioned building your own formula for wellbeing, resilience, and finding your purpose. Building your own smart formula, using tools that work for you—gratitude, a list of useful questions, additional exercises, meeting friends more regularly, meditation, helping someone in need—all help to improve resilience. When you're aware of the tools that work best for you—your own formula—you'll always have it to fall back on when you most need it.

Improve Your Day: Seven Ways

Procrastination is illogical from every viewpoint. It is like the man who wanted to cross the stream, so he sat on the bank to wait for all the water to run by.

—*There Is a Way Out,* Vernon Howard

What do successful, motivated, energetic people do to turn a bad day into a good one?

Everyone has bad days sometimes, right? However, when life seems to be full of days that are lacklustre, unproductive, and defeating, it's time to do something about it. Small actions (such as being grateful every day and the seven actions below) can make a big difference. It's all about taking these actions and creating new habits that work better for you. I read a newspaper headline recently in the *Irish Times* that really resonated with me: 'Exercise is a wonder drug, but you have to get off the couch to Benefit.'[10] It's about deciding what you'll change in your life, setting goals, and taking whatever action is necessary—adding gratitude, exercise, meditation or something that benefits you, to your day.

Even if you're not feeling down, the suggestions below are good practices. You can choose one or two and build up to seven. Or do all seven right now and start big!

The List of 7

1. *Right now*, say 'thank you'. List three to five things in your life that you really appreciate. If you're truly in the doldrums, you may be grateful for nothing more than the fact that you're now enjoying a rich cup of coffee or a lovely view. Or simply that you made it to work on time. Be specific and be thankful for something that is meaningful to you. The act of switching your brain to something positive—anything positive—on a regular basis has been proven to improve your days. Here's another benefit. When your brain is switched to positive, you're more productive.[11]
2. Exercise. Start with an exercise option that's easiest for you and build from there. If you're absolutely so short on time that you can't fit in 20–40 minutes, get up from your desk, and walk up and down a flight of stairs 10 times, or go outside and walk around the block. Then start your day again.
3. Make your next meal or snack a healthy, tasty, energy-giving one. Find a couple of healthy, delicious options that you enjoy and make sure you have the ingredients or snacks at home, when you're out running errands, or at work, so you don't reach for crisps or chocolate instead. It's no fun at all eating a healthy meal or snack just because it's good for you. Savouring/treating yourself to something tasty that you love will improve your day and your life in general.
4. Smile at a colleague and say something nice. We all love to receive a genuine compliment or bit of praise. Try saying something nice to someone now and see how it feels. Perhaps make an effort to speak to someone you don't normally talk

to, someone who may be new in your workplace or you know deep down may feel a little left out and would welcome an acknowledgement of their existence.

5. Get your least favourite piece of work out of the way, off your list, right now. With the task you're dreading out of the way, then you can spend the rest of your day doing something you like. Then you can spend the rest of your day doing stuff you like. You've just created a better day! If you can't make yourself tackle that least favourite piece of work right now, leave your desk, go for a walk around the office or outside the office, somewhere away from the task, then come back and get that piece of work done.
6. In the evening, write down *Five Thank You's* for good things in your life. Once more, be specific. This one is worth repeating at least twice a day.
7. Meditate. Even for a few minutes. Companies such as Google, Target, Apple, Nike, and so many more, are all investing in mindfulness and meditation for employees and seeing wellbeing benefits for everyone, including boosts in creativity and productivity.

Life goes by quickly. If the bad days are adding up, even if you only have one off day every month, that's 3.3 percent of your year. One off day every week is a staggering 14.3 percent of your time. If your company's manufacturing department, sales, marketing, or other division at work could close a productivity gap by 14 percent by implementing a few small changes, these changes would (and should) be implemented. Whether your off day happens during work or away from work, get out that gratitude journal and use it as your key to mindset change. If you're feeling uninspired more than 5 percent of the time, measure the time you're feeling off, and, take action on one or all of the seven steps above. You and those around you will benefit.

Part II

Routine 66: Your 66-Day Gratitude Habit Diary

The purpose of this 66-day diary is to start you on your own gratitude practice and to help you form a gratitude habit. The reason for the number of pages is that 66 days is the average found to form a new habit as per Philippa Lally's study (Chapter 1). I named the diary 'Your Routine 66 Gratitude-Habit Diary' as 'routine 66' evoked for me thoughts of a journey (and gratitude is a journey) along the historic Route 66 that runs from Chicago to Los Angeles, which seems very exciting, full of fun and joy. In my mind, I see blue skies, sunshine, and adventure. Sixty-six days of feeling grateful and documenting gratitude can take *your* mindset to a place where you feel life is exciting, fun, and joyful too.

When I read interesting books, especially ones that spark ideas, I often wish for additional pages in the books to journal, make notes, and write down random thoughts and ideas that come to mind in the moment. So I have created just that for you. My hope is that you use these following pages to make your own gratitude diary. Read the quotes. Notice the extra tips and reminders. Take the actions you need to problem-solve for yourself. Appreciate the good things in life as you journey towards your gratitude habit. The diary can be your master key to mindset change and help you design your own formula for wellbeing, resilience, success, and purpose.

In the diary, write a few lines on each page about what being grateful really means to you. As days go by, I suggest you notice how practicing gratitude is impacting your wellbeing. Continually ask yourself how you can continue to use gratitude to help your life?

Day 1

Reflect: Ask yourself, *What sparked my curiosity today?*

Today I am grateful for:

1. ______________________________

2. ______________________________

3. ______________________________

4. ______________________________

5. ______________________________

There are always flowers for those who want to see them.

—*Jazz,* Henri Matisse

Day 2

Action item: Ask yourself, *How am I feeling about setting off on my gratitude journey?* Notice and accept how you feel about it.

Today I am grateful for:

1. ______________________________

2. ______________________________

3. ______________________________

4. ______________________________

5. ______________________________

My socks may not match but my feet are always warm.

—Attributed to Maureen McCullough, Actor

Day 3

Action item: Ask yourself, *Who has helped me that I'd like to thank?* Then send a thank you note to that person.

Today I am grateful for:

1. ________________________________

2. ________________________________

3. ________________________________

4. ________________________________

5. ________________________________

I feel a very unusual sensation—if it's not indigestion, it must be gratitude.

—*Endymion*, Benjamin Disraeli

Day 4

Action item: Ask yourself, *What kind deed will I do for someone today?* Then do that kind deed for someone.

Today I am grateful for:

1. ______________________________

2. ______________________________

3. ______________________________

4. ______________________________

5. ______________________________

It's not happiness that brings us gratitude. It's gratitude that brings us happiness.

—Anonymous

Day 5

Action item: Ask yourself, *Who can I say thank you to today?* Then thank that person.

Today I am grateful for:

1. ________________________________

2. ________________________________

3. ________________________________

4. ________________________________

5. ________________________________

I was complaining that I had no shoes 'till I met a man who had no feet.

—Attributed to Confucius

Day 6

Action item: Ask yourself, *What might I do differently today as a result of my gratitude practice?* Then do it.

Today I am grateful for:

1. ____
2. ____
3. ____
4. ____
5. ____

"If you want to find happiness, find gratitude."

—*Unapologetically You: Reflections on Life and the Human Experience*, Steve Maraboli.

Day 7

Weekly check-in: How has writing down whatever you're grateful for worked for you this week?

Today I am grateful for:

1. ______________________________

2. ______________________________

3. ______________________________

4. ______________________________

5. ______________________________

Every blessing ignored becomes a curse.

—*The Alchemist,* Paulo Coelho

Day 8

Action item: Ask yourself, *How will I reward myself for completing eight days of my gratitude practice?* Then treat yourself.

Reward yourself for eight days on your gratitude journey.

Today I am grateful for:

1. ______________________________

2. ______________________________

3. ______________________________

4. ______________________________

5. ______________________________

"Enough" is a feast.

—Buddhist proverb

Day 9

Reflect: Ask yourself: *What did I learn today*?

Today I am grateful for:

1. ____________________

2. ____________________

3. ____________________

4. ____________________

5. ____________________

The only thing that ever sat its' [sic] *way to success is a hen.*

—Sarah Brown, Actress

Day 10

10-day check-in. What one thing appears most in your gratitude lists? Are you doing more of this?

Today I am grateful for:

1. ________________________

2. ________________________

3. ________________________

4. ________________________

5. ________________________

The way I see it, if you want the rainbow, you gotta put up with the rain.

—Dolly Parton, Twitter, 4 April 2013

Day 11

Reflect: Ask yourself, *What sparked my curiosity today?*

Today I am grateful for:

1. ____

2. ____

3. ____

4. ____

5. ____

Though I am grateful for the blessings of wealth, it hasn't changed who I am. My feet are still on the ground, I'm just wearing better shoes.

—*Independent on Sunday,* Oprah Winfrey

Day 12

Reflect: Ask yourself, *How am I* feeling *different as a result of developing my new gratitude habit?*

Today I am grateful for:

1. ____

2. ____

3. ____

4. ____

5. ____

The thing I'm most thankful for right now is elastic waistbands.

—Unknown

Day 13

Reflect: Ask yourself, *What am I doing differently today as a result of my gratitude practice?*

Today I am grateful for:

1. ______________________________

2. ______________________________

3. ______________________________

4. ______________________________

5. ______________________________

Silent gratitude isn't much use to anyone who has done a lot for you.

—Gladys Berthe Stern, Author

Day 14

Weekly check-in: How has writing down whatever you're grateful for worked for you this week?

Today I am grateful for:

1. ______________________________

2. ______________________________

3. ______________________________

4. ______________________________

5. ______________________________

Two kinds of gratitude: The sudden kind we feel for what we take; the larger kind we feel for what we give.

—*Captain Craig: A Book of Poems,* Edwin Arlington Robinson,

Day 15

Action item: Ask yourself, *What small kindness will I do for someone else right now?* Then do it.

Today I am grateful for:

1. ______________________________

2. ______________________________

3. ______________________________

4. ______________________________

5. ______________________________

A friend is someone who will bail you out of jail. A best friend is the one sitting next to you saying "'boy was that fun.'"

—Anonymous

Day 16

Action item: Ask yourself, *How will I reward myself for my continuing gratitude practice?* Then treat yourself.

Today I am grateful for:

1. ____________________

2. ____________________

3. ____________________

4. ____________________

5. ____________________

The most beautiful gift of nature is that it gives one pleasure to look around and try to comprehend what we see.

––—Albert Einstein

Day 17

Action item: Ask yourself, *What kindness will I show another today?* Then show someone that act of kindness.

Today I am grateful for:

1. ____________________

2. ____________________

3. ____________________

4. ____________________

5. ____________________

Let us remember that, as much has been given us, much will be expected from us, and that true homage comes from the heart as well as from the lips, and, shows itself in deeds."

—Thanksgiving Proclamation, 1901, Theodore Roosevelt

Day 18

Patterns, they're there to be noticed: Ask yourself, *What patterns are emerging in my gratitude? What will I do differently as a result of noticing these gratitude patterns?*

Today I am grateful for:

1. ____________________
2. ____________________
3. ____________________
4. ____________________
5. ____________________

Being regularly grateful for life's simple pleasures brings real joy
— Anonymous

Day 19

Action item: Reading through your gratitude lists to date, ask yourself, *What brings me most joy?* Then promise yourself to do more of these things.

Today I am grateful for:

1. ______________________________

2. ______________________________

3. ______________________________

4. ______________________________

5. ______________________________

What separates privilege from entitlement is gratitude.

—*Braving the Wilderness: The Quest for True Belonging and the Courage to Stand Alone,* Brené Brown

Day 20

Action item: Ask yourself, *What small kindness will I show someone else right now?* Then show someone that act of kindness.

Today I am grateful for:

1. ______________________________

2. ______________________________

3. ______________________________

4. ______________________________

5. ______________________________

If you are really thankful, what do you do? You share.

—Attributed to W. Clement Stone, American businessman, philanthropist, and author

Day 21

Weekly check-in: How has writing down whatever you're grateful for worked for you this week?

Today I am grateful for:

1. ______________________________

2. ______________________________

3. ______________________________

4. ______________________________

5. ______________________________

As we express our gratitude, we must never forget that the highest appreciation is not to utter words, but to live by them."

—Thanksgiving Day Proclamation, 1963,
John Fitzgerald Kennedy

Day 22

Reflect: Ask yourself, *What did I learn today? How will I use this learning to help me in future?*

Today I am grateful for:

1. ______________________________

2. ______________________________

3. ______________________________

4. ______________________________

5. ______________________________

Life is like riding a bicycle. To keep your balance you must keep moving.

—Letter to his son Eduard, February 5, 1930, Albert Einstein

Day 23

Action item: Ask yourself, *What kindness will I show another today?* Then show someone that act of kindness.

Today I am grateful for:

1. ______________________________

2. ______________________________

3. ______________________________

4. ______________________________

5. ______________________________

A thankful heart is not only the greatest virtue, but the parent of all the other virtues."

—*Oratio Pro Cnæo Plancio*, XXXIII, Cicero

Day 24

Reflect: As yourself, *How am I feeling different as a result of developing my new gratitude habit?*

Today I am grateful for:

1. ____________________

2. ____________________

3. ____________________

4. ____________________

5. ____________________

It was a woman that drove me to drink and I didn't have the decency to thank her.

—*Never Give a Sucker an Even Break,* WC Fields

Day 25

Patterns, they're there to be noticed. Ask yourself, *What patterns have emerged in my gratitude practice? What will I do differently as a result of noticing these gratitude patterns?*

Today I am grateful for:

1. ____
2. ____
3. ____
4. ____
5. ____

If you want to live a happy life, tie it to a goal, not to people or objects.

—Albert Einstein, *Einstein: A Centenary Volume*, by A.P. French

Day 26

Action item: Ask yourself, *What kindness will I show another today?* Then show someone that act of kindness.

Today I am grateful for:

1. ______________________________
2. ______________________________
3. ______________________________
4. ______________________________
5. ______________________________

Enjoy the little things in life for one day you'll look back and realize they were the big things

—Attributed to Kurt Vonnegut

Day 27

Relax: Close your eyes and take five deep calming breaths.

Today I am grateful for:

1. ______________________________

2. ______________________________

3. ______________________________

4. ______________________________

5. ______________________________

Give yourself a gift of five minutes of contemplation in awe of everything you see around you. Go outside and turn your attention to the many miracles around you. This five-minute-a-day regimen of appreciation and gratitude will help you to focus your life in awe.

—"A Perfect World," *Wayne's Blog*, Wayne Dyer

Day 28

Weekly check-in: How has writing down whatever you're grateful for worked for you this week?

Today I am grateful for:

1. ______________________________

2. ______________________________

3. ______________________________

4. ______________________________

5. ______________________________

When it comes to life the critical thing is whether you take things for granted or take them with gratitude.

—*The Autobiography of G. K. Chesterton*,
Gilbert K. Chesterton

Day 29

Action item: Ask yourself, *What kindness will I show another today?* Then show someone that act of kindness.

Today I am grateful for:

1. ________________________________

2. ________________________________

3. ________________________________

4. ________________________________

5. ________________________________

No one who achieves success does so without acknowledging the help of others. The wise and confident acknowledge this help with gratitude.

—Attributed to Alfred North Whitehead, English mathematician and philosopher

Day 30

Relax: Close your eyes and take five deep calming breaths.

Today I am grateful for:

1. ____

2. ____

3. ____

4. ____

5. ____

You never can tell whether bad luck may not after all turn out to be good luck.

—*A Roving Commission,* Winston Churchill

Day 31

Reflect: Ask yourself, *How am I feeling different as a result of developing my new gratitude habit? What will I do differently as a result of noticing these gratitude patterns?*

Today I am grateful for:

1. ______________________________

2. ______________________________

3. ______________________________

4. ______________________________

5. ______________________________

Gratitude is an opener of locked-up blessings.

—Marianne Williamson

Day 32

Patterns, they're there to be noticed: Ask yourself, *What am I doing differently as a result of noticing these gratitude-patterns?*

Today I am grateful for:

1. ____

2. ____

3. ____

4. ____

5. ____

The smallest act of kindness is worth more than the kindest intention.

—Attributed to Oscar Wilde

Day 33

Mid-way check-in. What one item appears most in your gratitude lists? Have you been doing more of this?

Today I am grateful for:

1. ____________________

2. ____________________

3. ____________________

4. ____________________

5. ____________________

That which does not kill us makes us stronger.

—*Twilight of the* Idols, Friedrich Wilhelm Nietzsche

Day 34

Reflect: Ask yourself: *What am I doing differently today as a result of my gratitude practice?*

Today I am grateful for:

1. ______________________________

2. ______________________________

3. ______________________________

4. ______________________________

5. ______________________________

Thank you for always being there for me even when I'm being a pain in the rear.

—Anonymous

Day 35

Weekly check-in. How has writing down whatever you're grateful for worked for you this week?

Today I am grateful for:

1. ______________________________

2. ______________________________

3. ______________________________

4. ______________________________

5. ______________________________

Happiness doesn't result from what we get, but from what we give.

—Ben Carson, Twitter, 29 October 2013

Day 36

Relax: Close your eyes and take five deep calming breaths.

Today I am grateful for:

1. ____

2. ____

3. ____

4. ____

5. ____

Stop now. Enjoy the moment. It's now or never.

—Maxime Lagacé, Twitter, 15 October 2019

Day 37

Action item: Ask yourself: *What kindness will I show another today?* Then show someone that act of kindness.

Today I am grateful for:

1. ______________________________

2. ______________________________

3. ______________________________

4. ______________________________

5. ______________________________

If you can find a path with no obstacles. it probably doesn't lead anywhere.

—*The Country Parson*, Frank A Clark

Day 38

Action item: Ask yourself, *Reading through my gratitude lists to date, what brings me most joy?* Then promise yourself to do more of these things.

Today I am grateful for:

1. ________________________________

2. ________________________________

3. ________________________________

4. ________________________________

5. ________________________________

He who has a why to live can bear almost any how.

—Friedrich Wilhelm Nietzsche

Day 39

Relax: Close your eyes and take five deep calming breaths.

Today I am grateful for:

1. ______________________________

2. ______________________________

3. ______________________________

4. ______________________________

5. ______________________________

Accept periods of suffering with gratitude, knowing that suffering can teach you very important lessons.

—Barbara Ann Kipfer

Day 40

Reflect: Ask yourself, *How am I feeling different as a result of developing my new gratitude habit?*

Today I am grateful for:

1. ____
2. ____
3. ____
4. ____
5. ____

Have gratitude for all that you have, and you can be happy exactly as you are.

—*Yogalosophy*, Mandy Ingber

Day 41

Reflect: Ask yourself, *What am I doing differently today as a result of my gratitude practice?*

Today I am grateful for:

1. ________________________________

2. ________________________________

3. ________________________________

4. ________________________________

5. ________________________________

Never bend your head. Always hold it high. Look the world straight in the face.

—Helen Keller

Day 42

Weekly check-in. How has writing down whatever you're grateful for worked for you this week?

Today I am grateful for:

1. ____

2. ____

3. ____

4. ____

5. ____

"Gratitude is the sign of noble souls."

—*Aesop's Fables*, Aesop

Day 43

Action item: Remind yourself of what's great about you. Acknowledge and appreciate your greatness.

Today I am grateful for:

1. ______________________________

2. ______________________________

3. ______________________________

4. ______________________________

5. ______________________________

Develop an attitude of gratitude, and give thanks for everything that happens to you, knowing that every step forward is a step toward achieving something bigger and better than your current situation.

—*Successful Selling,* Brian Tracy

Day 44

Patterns, they're there to be noticed: Ask yourself, *What am I doing differently as a result of noticing these gratitude-patterns?*

Today I am grateful for:

1. ____________________

2. ____________________

3. ____________________

4. ____________________

5. ____________________

Always remember people who have helped you along the way, and don't forget to lift someone up.

—Roy T. Bennett, Twitter, 10 November 2018

Day 45

Relax: Close your eyes and take five deep calming breaths.

Today I am grateful for:

1. ______________________________

2. ______________________________

3. ______________________________

4. ______________________________

5. ______________________________

Reflect upon your present blessings—of which every man has many—not on your past misfortunes, of which all men have some."

—*A Christmas Dinner*, Charles Dickens

Day 46

Action item: Ask yourself, *What kindness will I show another today?* Then show someone that act of kindness.

Today I am grateful for:

1. ______________________________

2. ______________________________

3. ______________________________

4. ______________________________

5. ______________________________

One can pay back the loan of gold, but one dies forever in debt to those who are kind.

—Malayan Proverb

Day 47

Reflect: Think about someone you love, someone you enjoy having in your life that you're grateful for.

Today I am grateful for:

1. ______________________________

2. ______________________________

3. ______________________________

4. ______________________________

5. ______________________________

I would like to thank my arms for always being by my side, my legs for always supporting me, and my fingers, because I can always count on them.

—Anonymous

Day 48

Reflect: Ask yourself, *What am I doing differently today as a result of my gratitude practice?*

Today I am grateful for:

1. ________________________________

2. ________________________________

3. ________________________________

4. ________________________________

5. ________________________________

This is a wonderful day. I've never seen it before.

—Maya Angelou, Twitter, 17 May 2013

Day 49

Weekly check-in: How has writing down whatever you're grateful for worked for you this week?

Today I am grateful for:

1. ______________________________

2. ______________________________

3. ______________________________

4. ______________________________

5. ______________________________

When I started counting my blessings, my whole life turned around.

—*The Tao of Willie: A Guide to the Happiness in Your Heart*, Willie Nelson

Day 50

Relax: Close your eyes and take five deep calming breaths.

Today I am grateful for:

1. ______________________________

2. ______________________________

3. ______________________________

4. ______________________________

5. ______________________________

You've always believed in me. Thank you!

—Anonymous

Day 51

Action item: Ask yourself, *What kindness will I show another today?* And show someone that act of kindness.

Today I am grateful for:

1. ______________________________________

2. ______________________________________

3. ______________________________________

4. ______________________________________

5. ______________________________________

Gratitude is simply a deep and genuine sense of appreciation for what you have in your life. For things big and small. For the air you breathe; the unconditional love of your pet; for blessing of someone who loves you.

—"The Most Powerful Gratitude Practice You're Not Doing," Marie Forleo

Day 52

Check-in: What one thing appears most in my gratitude lists?
Am I doing more of this?

Today I am grateful for:

1. ______________________________

2. ______________________________

3. ______________________________

4. ______________________________

5. ______________________________

There is always, always, always something to be thankful for.

—Anonymous

Day 53

Relax: Close your eyes, take five deep calming breaths.

Today I am grateful for:

1. ______________________________

2. ______________________________

3. ______________________________

4. ______________________________

5. ______________________________

It is not joy that makes us grateful; it is gratitude that makes us joyful.

—TEDGlobal, 2013, David Steindl-Rast

Day 54

Action item: Ask yourself, *What kindness will I show another today?* Then show someone that act of kindness.

Today I am grateful for:

1. ______________________________

2. ______________________________

3. ______________________________

4. ______________________________

5. ______________________________

You cannot do a kindness too soon because you never know how soon it will be too late.

—*The Conduct of Life,* Ralph Waldo Emerson

Day 55

Reflect: Ask yourself, *What am I doing differently today as a result of my gratitude practice?*

Today I am grateful for:

1. ____

2. ____

3. ____

4. ____

5. ____

To sit at one's table on a sunny morning, with four clear hours of uninterruptible security, plenty of nice white paper, and a Squeezer pen - that is true happiness.

—Winston Churchill

Day 56

Weekly check-in: How has writing down whatever you're grateful for worked for you this week?

Today I am grateful for:

1. ______________________________

2. ______________________________

3. ______________________________

4. ______________________________

5. ______________________________

Presents are made for the pleasure of who gives them, not the merits of who receives them."

The Shadow of the Wind, Carlos Ruiz Zafón

Day 57

Action item: Reading through your gratitude lists to date, ask yourself, *What brings me the most joy?* Then vow to do more of these things.

Today I am grateful for:

1. ______________________________

2. ______________________________

3. ______________________________

4. ______________________________

5. ______________________________

For it is in giving that we receive."

—Prayer of Saint Francis, Saint Francis of Assisi

Day 58

Relax: Close your eyes and take five deep calming breaths.

Today I am grateful for:

1. ______________________________

2. ______________________________

3. ______________________________

4. ______________________________

5. ______________________________

Maybe you have to know darkness before you can appreciate the light.

—Madeleine L'Engle

Day 59

Action item: Ask yourself, *What kindness will I show another today?* Then show someone that act of kindness.

Today I am grateful for:

1. ____

2. ____

3. ____

4. ____

5. ____

I'm thankful for my struggle because without it I wouldn't have stumbled across my strength."

—Alexandra Elle, Twitter, 28 November 2013

Day 60

Patterns, they're there to be noticed: Ask yourself, *What am I doing differently as a result of noticing these gratitude-patterns?*

Today I am grateful for:

1. ____

2. ____

3. ____

4. ____

5. ____

We can only be said to be alive in those moments when our hearts are conscious of our treasures

—Spoken by Chrysis, *The Woman of Andros,* Thorton Wilder

Day 61

Relax: Close your eyes and take five deep calming breaths.

Today I am grateful for:

1. ______________________________

2. ______________________________

3. ______________________________

4. ______________________________

5. ______________________________

Now and then it's good to pause in our pursuit of happiness and just be happy." –

—Attributed to Guillaume Apollinaire, French poet, playwright, and novelist

Day 62

Reflect: Ask yourself, *What am I doing differently today as a result of my gratitude practice?*

Today I am grateful for:

1. ____________________________

2. ____________________________

3. ____________________________

4. ____________________________

5. ____________________________

The golden way is to be friends with the world and to regard the whole human family as one.

—*The Encyclopaedia of Gandhian Thoughts*,
Mahatma Gandhi

Day 63

Weekly check-in: How has writing down whatever you're grateful for worked for you this week?

Today I am grateful for:

1. ______________________

2. ______________________

3. ______________________

4. ______________________

5. ______________________

God gave you a gift of 86,400 seconds today. Have you used one to say 'thank you'?

—William Arthur Ward

Day 64

Relax: Close your eyes and take five deep calming breaths.

Today I am grateful for:

1. ________________________________

2. ________________________________

3. ________________________________

4. ________________________________

5. ________________________________

Gratitude unlocks the fullness of life. It turns what we have into enough, and more. It turns denial into acceptance, chaos to order, confusion to clarity. It can turn a meal into a feast, a house into a home, a stranger into a friend.

—The Language of Letting Go: Hazelden Meditation Series, Melody Beattie

Day 65

Reflect: Ask yourself, *How am I feeling different as a result of developing my new gratitude habit?*

Today I am grateful for:

1. ____________________

2. ____________________

3. ____________________

4. ____________________

5. ____________________

At times our own light goes out and is rekindled by a spark from another person. Each of us has cause to think with deep gratitude of those who have lighted the flame within us.

—Attributed to Albert Schweitzer, German philosopher, Nobel Peace Prize winner

Day 66

Action item: Ask yourself, *How will I ensure I continue with my new habits?* Write down your thoughts and review as often as you need to keep these positive habits.

Today I am grateful for:

1. ______________________________

2. ______________________________

3. ______________________________

4. ______________________________

5. ______________________________

No one who achieves success does so without acknowledging the help of others. The wise and confident acknowledge this help with gratitude.

—Attributed to Alfred North Whitehead, English mathematician and philosopher

Reflect: Ask yourself these questions: *What beneficial habits did I develop during the last 66 days? How are these habits working out for me? What's better in my life now compared with before I began my gratitude practice?*

Create Your Own Gratitude Formula to Improve Your Mindset

For 66 days—at least once each day—you have written down five things you're grateful for. Now review your answers to determine which items appear most often, then enter the top five in the first column below. Next, complete the rest of the template to create your gratitude formula. After 66 days, you'll have a lifelong record of things you're grateful for—a fabulous reminder to refer to anytime you need a boost.

My Gratitude Formula: Template

Top 5 things I'm grateful for	What benefits do these 5 things bring to my life?	What will I do more of? This is your Formula	Measure weekly (1–5) how I'm doing. (1= not good–5 = great)

Top 5 things I'm grateful for	What benefits do these 5 things bring to my life?	What will I do more of? This is your Formula	Measure weekly (1–5) how I'm doing. (1= not good–5 = great)

Random Thoughts and Ideas to Reinforce Gratitude and Spark Creativity

Use these pages to record notes, lists, special moments—perhaps even your favourite gratitude quotes. These are your pages to use as you wish.

Breathe to Bring a Sense of Calm

To end this book, I share this breathing practice with you in the hope that you'll take a moment to read it, try it, relax, feel the sentiment—experience a moment of calm.

Breathing out for longer than breathing in, can calm the breath, body and mind.

Close your eyes.

Bring your attention to your breath.

Take a deep breath in through the nose and a deep breath out through the mouth.

Keep focusing your attention on your breath.

Next breathe in through the nose for a count of 5–7 and breathe out through the nose for a count of 7–11.

You can choose the number, so long as the out-breath is longer.

If you feel overwhelmed, or simply would enjoy a moment of peace and relaxation, breathing like this for even a few minutes may bring you a sense of space and calm.

***

Thank you for reading this book. I hope that what you've learned here, working on your diary—and journaling after the sixty-six days—brings you a better life, more resilience, contentment, and many moments of pure joy.

Notes

1 Phillippa Lally, Cornelia H. M. Van Jaarsveld, Henry W. W. Potts, and Jane Wardle, "How Are Habits Formed: Modelling Habit Formation in the Real World." *European Journal of Social Psychology* 40, no. 6 (2009): 998–1009. https://doi.org/10.1002/ejsp.674.

2 George J Ziogas, "How Gratitude Rewires Your Brain And How To Make It Work for You," *Medium*, December 10, 2019, https://medium.com/change-your-mind/how-gratitude-rewires-your-brain-and-how-to-make-it-work-for-you-894e8bf73c59.

3 Claire D Clarke, "How Gratitude Actually Changes Your Brain and Is Good for Business" *Thrive Global*, February 7, 2019, https://thriveglobal.com/stories/how-gratitude-actually-changes-your-brain-and-is-good-for-business/.

4 Mark Murphy, "Neuroscience Explains Why You Need To Write Down Your Goals If You Actually Want to Achieve Them," *Forbes*, April 15, 2018, https://www.forbes.com/sites/markmurphy/2018/04/15/neuroscience-explains-why-you-need-to-write-down-your-goals-if-you-actually-want-to-achieve-them/.

5 Marshall Goldsmith, Mark Reiter, and Shane Clester, *What Got You Here Won't Get You There* (London: Profile Books, 2012, Kindle Location 2810).

6 Rachel Hartman, *Seraphina* (City published: Publisher, 2012) Page number necessary?

7 Leslie Riopel, "Resilience Skills, Factors and Strategies of the Resilient Person," *PositivePsychology.com*, April 29, 2020, https://positivepsychology.com/resilience-skills/.

8 Ed O'Brian, "The Joy of Giving Lasts Longer Than the Joy of Getting," *Association for Psychological Science,* December 20, 2018, https://www.psychologicalscience.org/news/releases/the-joy-of-giving.html.

9 Alvin Powell, "When Science Meets Mindfulness: Harvard Researchers Study How It Seems to Change the Brain in Depressed Patients," *The Harvard Gazette*, April 9, 2019, https://news.harvard.edu/gazette/story/2018/04/harvard-researchers-study-how-mindfulness-may-change-the-brain-in-depressed-patients/.

10 Padraig O'Morain, "Exercise Is a Wonder Drug, but You Have to Get off the Couch to Benefit," *The Irish Times,* February 21, 2017, https://www.irishtimes.com/life-and-style/health-family/exercise-is-a-wonder-drug-but-you-have-to-get-off-the-couch-to-benefit-1.2976420.

11 Phil Drazewski,"Benefits of a Happy Brain: Positive Employees Are More Productive Employees," *The Predictive Index,* March 4, 2020, https://www.predictiveindex.com/blog/benefits-of-a-happy-brain-positive-employees-are-more-productive-employees/

Acknowledgements

I am grateful to my husband, Niall, for once again encouraging me to write, and for believing I could produce something that can help others. I appreciate his 'thinking-big' attitude and his helping me not to let anything get in my way.

I'm grateful every day for my daughter, Holly; more grateful than words can ever fully express. I'm especially grateful for the hugs—always top of my gratitude list.

Thank you so much to my editor, Kelly Malone, who, once again, challenged and supported me to do my very best. As Kelly (who also edited my best-selling book *The Formula: How to be your very best self*) is based in Seattle and I'm in Ireland, we once again had a wonderful 24-hour operation going. And we enjoyed working together once more. Thank you, too, to Lisa Tener, author and book writing coach, for recommending Kelly as my editor initially and for her ongoing wisdom.

I would also like to thank Conor Duggan for his help with the title and chapter titles, quote-sourcing, his read-through of the first draft, and his ideas and suggestions. Conor himself is a wonderful storyteller, a recipient of the Marian Keyes Young Writers Award. I have no doubt that if he decides to write a book in the future it will be best-seller material.

Thank you to Orla Kelly, Orla Kelly publishing. I really enjoyed working with you on the book cover and interior design.

A final thank you to all the people who listened to me, including Mary Rose Burke and Bronagh McDonald. You have helped me make this book, workbook and journal possible.

About the Author

Maria Burke is bestselling author of *The Formula-How to be your very best self.*

She holds a BSc in Pharmacy from Trinity College, Dublin, Ireland, an advanced diploma in Executive Coaching and a certificate in Cognitive Behavioural Therapy.

Maria owned and managed three retail pharmacies and, later, ran her own wholesale and distribution business, working with leading global brands, including OPI, St. Tropez, Neal's Yard Remedies and Smashbox Cosmetics.

Whether you wish to alleviate stress in your life, have come to a crossroads and desire direction, or yearn for advancement both personally and professionally, the techniques in this book will help you transform your outlook and unlock your potential.

Maria lives in Dublin with her husband and daughter.

You can connect with Maria at https://www.waywordsjournals.com.

www.ingramcontent.com/pod-product-compliance
Lightning Source LLC
Chambersburg PA
CBHW070511200726
48293CB00007B/2488

* 9 7 8 1 9 9 9 3 6 6 0 2 5 *